God Is Real

My Spiritual Journey to God and Eternity

Published by Shelley Joy Gilbert
Ossining, New York 10562 USA
Email: shelley@shelleyjoygilbert.com
Website: www.shelleyjoygilbert.com

ISBN No. 978-0-9718317-9-7

Digitally printed in the United States by CreateSpace
Covers and Interior designed by Shelley Gilbert
Cover Image: Sal Gaetano

God Is Real

My Spiritual Journey to God and Eternity

Shelley Gilbert

Shelley Gilbert's Other Books

Fiction

Land of Sooj, Six Seahorse Stories, 2011
Swimming Naked with Jellyfish, 2008

Nonfiction

Islands, A Coloring Book for Adults, 2nd Edition, 30 Hand-Drawn Drawings, 30 Poems, 2011
Islands, A Coloring Book for Adults, Volume 2, 30 Hand-Drawn Drawings, 30 Poems, 2011
Islands, A Coloring Book for Teens and Kids, 30 Hand-Drawn Drawings, 30 Poems and Recipes, 2010
Islands, A Coloring Book for Adults, 30 Drawings, 30 Poems, 2001

To Hank, Into Eternity

CHAPTERS

CHAPTER 1
Bed, Bath and Beyond

For the first 59 years of my life, I was an atheist. My parents didn't raise me to be an atheist. They just didn't bring God or a spiritual life into our home.

I didn't mind being an atheist. I was always independent and relied upon myself anyway, so I didn't feel the need to lean on anyone else. And I loved the heated debates I had with people about God. My favorite lines to stump the believers were: "*If God created the world, who created God?*" and "*Can you prove there's a God?*" I was very black and white then. If you couldn't prove things to me, I didn't believe. And I didn't believe in a spiritual world or in anything that had to do with it, like ghosts, so it was easier and neater to just disregard the whole thing.

One day when I was 55 years of age, my life shifted into a new direction. This is a funny and ironic story. I was shopping in my local Bed, Bath and Beyond store, buying yet another set of bed linens because I didn't have that particular shade of beige. I suddenly stopped walking and looked down at all the stuff in my cart and felt a longing. I silently implored: *Is this it? Is this all there is to life?* That Peggy Lee song came into my head: *Is That All There Is?* I just stood there, in that store, staring at all my stuff in the cart, and feeling a strong yearning to find a deeper meaning to life. I couldn't believe that life was just about cooking dinners, buying bed linens and sending out greeting cards. I didn't realize then that I wanted to find God. I just wanted to find something deeper and more meaningful. Eternal Being does indeed have an ironic sense of humor when It planted that seed in me in Bed, Bath and *Beyond*.

At some point soon after that shopping experience, the second seed came into my conscious brain. I had seen Rose Kennedy being interviewed on TV after her son, President John F. Kennedy, was assassinated. The reporter asked how she coped with all her difficult times. The camera went in close on Rose Kennedy's face as she answered. She cocked her head, had this serene look on her face and said that it was her faith that got her through. I remember looking at her peaceful face then and thinking, *I want that face.* I wanted what was in her heart, what was in her being that emanated such a peaceful look. Growing up with anxious and depressed parents, I didn't often see that face in my childhood home. Rose Kennedy's face came back into my awareness as the goal of my spiritual journey.

I made an appointment with the rabbi at my local temple in New York. I told her I wanted to find God and asked her for help. She said I should go every Friday night to temple service, go every Saturday morning to Torah Study, plan to become bat mitzvahed, and read the *Holy Scriptures* and a book on Jewish heritage. I did as she said for about a year. Nothing happened. I didn't feel that I found God or even that I was on the right track. It didn't matter to me that billions of people on Earth said they believed in God. I had to *know* God. It wasn't good enough to just *say* that I believed in God. I had to *feel* God. So I stopped doing all the things the rabbi told me to do and I stopped going to temple. I felt I was going in the wrong direction.

CHAPTER 2
The Tornado Ghost

On January 12, 2002 something pivotal happened that enabled me to open my mind to believe in God. My husband Hank and I were staying at a historic, antique-filled bed and breakfast house in Connecticut. It was Saturday night and we went to sleep on the comfortable and luxurious bed.

In the middle of the night, I woke up, eyes wide open, and sat up tall in bed. Looking back on this experience, I must have looked like I was in one of those movies when someone is under a spell and rises from their sleep with their eyes wide open, back straight as a board. I didn't hear or smell anything and I wasn't touched by anything but I instantly turned my head to the left.

About three feet away from me, suspended in mid air about eye level to me, was a ghost. The ghost was shaped like a huge, round, horizontal Bayer aspirin tablet. It was flat on the top and bottom with rounded edges. It was about two feet in diameter. The ghost was made up of thousands of tiny black particles, each shaped like a sperm, which furiously rotated clockwise as fast as a tornado. It spun around so violently that it spewed off some of the tiny black particles. But, although the ghost was just a few feet away and although it was spinning furiously, I didn't feel a breeze and none of the particles touched me. It was as if the ghost was contained in its own little world, separate from my human world.

This whole experience actually lasted just a few seconds, because as soon as I sat up and turned my head and my eyes saw the ghost, as if it saw me looking at it, it broke down into an amoebic mob of particles and made a mad dash for the closed old door and disappeared through the warped frame's long crack.

I sat up for a while thinking about this experience. Strangely, I did not *feel* fear because if I did, I would have awakened my husband. I did feel a sort of fear because I didn't want to put my head back down on the pillow, afraid to go back to sleep, afraid the ghost would return. But I was very tired and lay back down to ponder what I should do. The next thing I knew, it was morning.

As soon as we woke up, I told Hank about the ghost. He just listened to me. He looked like he was believing me. I told him there probably was a small chance it was all a dream but I didn't think so. It didn't feel like a dream. It felt real and I remembered it in vivid detail.

When we went downstairs for breakfast, I was so excited that I told everyone in the dining room what happened to me that night. The two owners mockingly pooh-poohed my story but there was a visiting pastor from Pennsylvania. She also stayed overnight because she was to give a sermon at a nearby church. She confirmed that she was also visited by the ghost. She said she didn't see what I saw but she woke up during the night and felt its presence sitting in a chair by her bed. She said that in her line of work, people often come to her with stories and issues concerning ghosts and spirits. With the pastor as witness, I was validated 100% that I did indeed see a ghost. Actually, I think this pastor was an Angel because in the days ahead I tried to reach her but I couldn't find her anywhere, even though she gave me her business card.

Seeing the ghost was a shocking but crucial experience. It had served a greater purpose in my life than just to amaze me. It took about a year to digest and process the ghost before I could tell anyone else. Then I told a friend. After getting this experience out, I started to really think about the ghost. It dawned on me that *I saw a ghost!* The reality of seeing a ghost, I realized, became proof that there really was a spiritual world. Standing now on the threshold of this whole new world, my mind looked out and wondered: *Wow! Now that I know ghosts are real, what else can I believe in?* The answer came in my very next breath: *God.* But, still, I didn't find God for another couple years. And on that day, everything became crystal clear.

CHAPTER 3
Who Moved?

I was in my car running errands that hot sunny afternoon in late July 2004. It was just another ordinary day, or so I thought. As I was lazily making my left turn at the corner of South State Road and Pleasantville Road in Briarcliff Manor, New York, I glanced to my right, as I always did, to read the wise saying posted on the sign in front of Briarcliff Congregational Church. The sign on the lawn said:

"You say there's distance between you and God. Who moved?"

Those words stopped me dead in my tracks. I stopped my car and stared at those words. I found myself thinking about what those words meant.

Suddenly I began to whisper the answer to the sign:

I moved. It must be me who moved because God doesn't move. He's all around us.

Then I thought about what I was saying.

Why am I answering? I don't believe in God.

I suddenly felt so utterly lonely, like there was black all around me and I was all alone in the Universe. I began to cry and shake. I didn't know what was happening to me. I remember thinking that I could stop this strange feeling by just taking off in my car and continuing down the road into Pleasantville to run my errands, but I decided to stay with the feeling. I was oblivious to the line of cars piling up behind me, honking their horns. Then I suddenly heard their horns and I realized I had to move. I looked around me and saw that the small Briarcliff Public Library with its big, empty parking lot was just a few feet away, so I pulled into a spot in the quietest corner of the lot and parked my car. I turned the engine off and just sat there crying and shaking.

I don't remember feeling afraid or puzzled. Somehow I was trusting whatever was taking me over. Without thinking, I looked down at my chest and saw that my chest was ethereally opening up and that a small current of wavy air was going into me. A serene feeling began to wash over me. Then God began to play a game of connect the spiritual dots with me. visions and signs that I had experienced in my past, some of which I forgot for decades, came alive again in my mind.

I thought about the ghost and how it proved to me there really was a spiritual world. Then I remembered a traumatic experience I had when I was about five years old. My beloved father had just left our home, abandoning me, which threw me in a state of panic and chaos. My older sister, who hated me, had bonded with my mother, so they were aligned and spent time together. But I aligned with my father and now that he was gone, I was alone. He and my mother were divorcing. My father suffered from severe depression and anxiety and my mother couldn't take care of him and two little girls.

I developed signs of trauma: muscle ticks, bedwetting, nailbiting, nightmares, hallucinations. One day I was leaving our sixth floor apartment to visit a neighbor. I opened the front door but I stood on the threshold and couldn't go any further. I looked down the dark hallway but I couldn't take a step out onto the hallway floor. Even though I walked down this dark hallway many, many times before, on that day I couldn't move. I was physically paralyzed. I couldn't even turn around and go back into my house. I just stood there unable to move in any direction. My mind wanted to move but I couldn't get my body to move. Then a strange thing happened. I saw an ethereal cocoon begin to wrap itself around me, starting at my feet, going up and stopping at my neck. My whole body, including my arms, was wrapped in this mummy-like cocoon. It made me feel safe and secure. It calmed me down. Then I got an idea how to break out of the trauma and paralysis. I put out my arms and twirled off the threshold. Then I twirled all the way down the long hallway. The trauma was over but I picked up a new habit and twirled in our home and in the street for a long time after. I feel that Holy Spirit came to me on that day to protect and help me.

Connecting another dot, I thought about that day in 1974 when I was 29. I was feeling pretty despondent at that time, having spent four years trying to make a living as a visual artist in Manhattan but failing. Not knowing how else to support myself, I enlisted in the Army. My sister was married to an Army officer and I was envious of her free health care and general protection from life. But as the day of my enlistment grew near, I was becoming increasingly anxious and fearful. I was a free spirit and knew I would hate losing my freedom and someone telling me what to do all the time. But if I didn't go, I wouldn't know how to take care of myself. I was stuck in a tight spot.

Two days before the big day, I was sitting on my bed, staring out into my room, not knowing which way to turn. It was daytime. With the suddenness of a light just turned on, a brilliant white, round glow with a more brilliant Christian cross in the middle of the glow appeared before my eyes. The vision was suspended in mid air. The glow and cross were about ten inches tall and sat about eight feet in front of me, a little lower than my eye level. The light that emanated from the glow was contained. There weren't any rays like you see in some movies. The whole cross fit totally within the glow. It was a plain, elegant cross with no detail. The ends of the narrow vertical and horizontal bars were cut straight across.

Although the glow and cross were as intensely bright as a flame, I stared easily into it. I wasn't afraid by its presence or doubted what was before my eyes. I never said to myself, *What is this?* or *Why is a Christian cross coming to me? I'm Jewish!* Actually, my mind was blank, without any thoughts. But I was transfixed by this incredible sight, spiritually locked into it. It was the same spiritually locked-in feeling that I had when I saw the ghost. I was aware that the glow and cross were calming me down, making me feel peaceful and serene. I remember how the glow and cross came on but I don't remember how they went away. After staring at it for a while, I think I probably put my head down on a pillow and went to sleep because the next thing I knew, I was awakening from sleep. The vision was no longer there but I didn't even remember that I saw it! Actually, I didn't remember this event until 30 years later, when I was sitting in my car experiencing my epiphany.

I didn't decide that day if I should go into the Army but when the day came to report for duty, I made the crystal clear decision not to go. I showed up at Fort Hamilton in Brooklyn and had to claw my way out of the Army. I was fighting with a male officer who refused to let me go, when a female officer came to my rescue and gave me an Honorable Discharge. I remember her telling me that if I didn't want the Army, the Army didn't want me. Made sense to me.

Another spiritual experience happened when I was studying to be an artist in Lower Manhattan. I was working on a collage. It was filled with hundreds of cut-out pictures. I was at the end of the design and I couldn't figure out how to end it. I worked for a long time trying to find the right picture and where to place the last piece, when a tiny little square suddenly flipped over to reveal the whole face of a high-spirited, happy woman. Her face was perfect. That was just how I felt about my art, excited. And the size of the little square fit perfectly in the spot that ended the design. Now some people might call this a coincidence but I know that Eternal Being helped me out.

Back to sitting in my car... I thought about smaller spiritual signs I experienced. Like when I was a teen, I used to call my mother the Jewish Jesus Christ because she was so compassionate and giving and would give even to those who hurt her...I always liked churches and felt spiritual and serene in their sanctuaries. I didn't feel that way in synagogues...The number 3 has always been my favorite. It's a profound number, as in Father, Son, Holy Spirit.

As the last spiritual dot was connected, a floodgate opened and all the Truth came pouring out. I suddenly realized: *It's all true. There really is a spiritual world. There really is a God. Jesus really is the Son of God. The Bible really is true. I really was saved by God when I was 5 and 29 years of age.* I felt resolute in all this decision making. There wasn't a doubt in my mind. I was Jewish for the first 59 years of my life but in the heat of all that spiritual awakening, in my heart I converted to Christianity on the spot. I knew God wanted me to be Christian. In the half hour that I sat in my car, I went from believing nothing to believing everything.

CHAPTER 4
NOW!

When I got home, I was all excited. I told Hank about my experience. He just listened to me at first, taking in all that I was telling him. In the weeks ahead when he saw I was serious, he became a little angry. When we met we were happy little atheists but now I was filled with God and shifting away from Hank. Maybe he feared I would leave him. But Hank stayed by my side and his fear slowly melted away.

I wanted to join a church. I wanted to study the Bible. I wanted to go to school and take Christianity 101 courses and learn all about Jesus. But I wanted to do all of that *NOW!* I was frustrated when I realized I couldn't. The most immediate thing I could do was to buy books on the subject.

I went to my local Barnes & Noble and looked at some Christian books. I didn't feel right with them. I didn't understand the words, the concepts, the history. Then I realized that I didn't know anything about God or Christianity or religions or the Bible. I was like a baby, a young child first learning this huge, deep subject. I stopped in the aisle and thought, *If a mother was teaching her little daughter about God and Christianity, how would she do it?* I answered, *She would go to the children's section of a book store and buy her daughter some books.* So I went over to the children's section. Excitedly, I told the saleswoman what I was doing and could she please show me where those books were. She took me to the spiritual section. I bought eight *first* books: how to pray, who is God?, a coffee-table family Bible filled with pictures, a book on Christianity, a daily devotional book, and a few others. I couldn't wait to get them home!

I was in ecstasy, looking at all the books at home and trying to decide which one to read first. The books were sprawled all over my couch and coffee table. I could barely contain my excitement. I read a few pages of one book and then picked up another and read a few pages, and then picked up another. I kept going back and forth because I didn't have the patience to sit and read just one book.

Then I wanted to join a church, so I went online to explore my local churches. It suddenly dawned on me, the gravity of what I was about to do. I was a Jew who wanted to join a Christian church. I thought about the Jewish groups who believed in Jesus so I called them to see if I belonged there. I spoke to a man at Jews for Jesus. He explained what their organization was about. He asked me to come down for a visit but I backed off. I didn't feel that was right for me. Then I learned a member of the Messianic Jews lived nearby so I went over for a visit. The man was calling Jesus by a Hebrew name and that turned me off. He was talking about Jesus from a Jewish point of view and, somehow, that turned me off too, so I knew the Messianic Jews wasn't for me.

I remember sitting at my kitchen table and thinking about all this. I felt a deep, unmistakable need to uproot my roots from my Jewish religion and plant new roots into new Christian soil. That's what I wanted to do. That's what I felt God wanted me to do. For the first couple of years, I was unsettled in my new and complicated identity, but in due time I grew to understand that my heritage was Jewish but my religion and spirituality were now Christian.

I went online again to explore local churches. The artist, the romantic in me wanted a church with a big white spire that I had seen in so many of those wonderful classic movies. I was looking for one in my neighborhood when, suddenly, Holy Spirit planted a picture in the right side of my brain behind my ear of the church in Briarcliff whose sign connected me to God. *Of course, I must go there.* I went onto their site and read all about Briarcliff Congregational Church.

I went to their Sunday service. In my state of excitation, I became a member that very day. I signed up to work on a couple committees. I went to service every Sunday. I joined their Bible Study group. I wrote a rapturous song about the church. I offered to start and organize their first art and craft holiday fair. And I told them all about my epiphany in front of their directory sign. It was strange, because I noticed that every time I told my story, I felt chills in my body. I was in love with God. For the first six months since my epiphany, I was so filled with a high energy that I felt I could move mountains. I was baptized there on February 6, 2005.

As I was learning about God and Christianity, I was becoming more and more orthodox. I was believing every word in the Bible and looking for more epiphanies and signs from God. This Protestant church had Holy Communion only the first Sunday of the month but I was wanting it every Sunday. I even resented that they served grape juice instead of wine. We didn't go up to the altar to receive communion but stayed in our seats and that bothered me too. I wanted it all to be authentic. As I was learning about Jesus's human family, I found this Protestant church was emphasizing Joseph and ignoring Mary. But I wanted to learn about *all* of His family. At that time, I didn't get that there was politics in religion, that the Catholic Church revered Mary but the Protestant Church tended to play up Joseph. After a year of going to this church, something told me to move on and find a more religious church.

CHAPTER 5
Beth

At about this time I heard about a spiritual direction program offered by Mariandale Retreat in Ossining, NY. I needed someone to talk to, like a spiritual therapist. When I learned that Mariandale was a Catholic institution, I was wary if an individualist feminist like me could fit into their program and if I could find someone I would feel comfortable with to talk to. I felt their agenda would perhaps overtly or covertly tow the Catholic line and they would try to influence me but I was wrong. I spent the next two years meeting once a month with Beth. *Call me Beth*, she said, *not Sister.* I loved Beth the first time I met with her and felt totally comfortable with her. She never brought the dogmas of Catholicism into our meetings. She let me talk as I wished, cry when I needed, accepted me as I was and wasn't judgmental in any way. She was a literature professor and I was an author, so we were connected by words. And by our love for God. Beth was gentle with me. She nudged me to pray when I was lost or confused. She made easy, thoughtful suggestions when I needed them. She believed me when I told her about the signs and visions I received from God. I think I stopped going to Beth just after I started *A Course in Miracles*, which I'll tell you about later. I told her about this program but she said she never heard of it. I brought her the book to look at and told her that Jesus channeled His words through a scribe. She cautiously looked at a page or two and then put it down.

When I found *A Course in Miracles*, I felt that I had reached the end of the road with Beth. I saw her one or two more times just to be sure. I felt right about leaving the program at that time. It's just about moving on.

CHAPTER 6
Glass Pebble Cross

I'd like to tell you about several additional signs, visions and knowings I've experienced in recent years.

On August 20, 2006, Holy Spirit visited me. I was making beaded jewelry that I sold at different outlets. I finished a line of bracelets and cleared off my beading table. I put away all my beads to make room for a new line of bracelets I wanted to make. I walked away from the table but when I returned, I saw in the middle of the cleaned-off area a Christian cross made up of small, clear glass pebbles. You know, the kind that were rounded like a half-moon on one side and flat on the other side. I like these clear glass pebbles and kept a glass of them on my beading table. The cross was positioned on the table askew but its lines were absolutely perfectly straight. The long part of the cross was made up of all one side of the pebbles while the short part was made up of the other side. I stood there and just stared at the glass cross. For the first few seconds, I was in a mild state of shock, just staring at the cross. Then I knew where it came from. Hank was working in his office and I called him in. I pointed to the cross and asked if he did this, knowing that he didn't but I just wanted to eliminate all possibilities. He stared at the cross and said no. I told him I didn't do it either. I told him Holy Spirit did it. He didn't say anything about this. We looked at it some more and then Hank went back to work. I tried to Crazy Glue the glass pebbles together to keep it as it was but the round glass pebbles wouldn't hold together. I put the pebbles in a pretty silk sack and I keep it together with my other signs from God. I went to my spiritual journal and recorded this experience, like I did with all the others.

During the summer of 2006, Hank and I were at an outdoor party. We had met this group of people the year before, so they were new to us. It was a sunny day and I was talking to a very suntanned man everyone called Mike the Painter, to distinguish him from all the other Mikes.

While I was talking to Mike, his whole face suddenly turned a deathly gray color. It happened in a snap, as if you turned on a light and *boom!* It was shocking to see this change and my brain took a few seconds before I realized that his face color had turned to gray. His face was gray for several seconds and then it snapped back to his normal tan color. I stood there staring at him. I don't remember what he was saying.

A day or two later I understood what I saw and why I saw it. Mike was a heavy smoker. He was usually smoking a cigarette whenever I saw him. I believed that God wanted me to warn Mike to stop smoking or he'll pass on young.

I waited a whole year before I got up the courage to tell Mike. I didn't want this new group of friends to think I was a religious zealot or crazy. So that summer I went up to Mike and told him what I saw and that I was meant to pass this warning on to him. I apologized if he thought I was a zealot but Mike stopped me and said he was Catholic and believed that people do see signs from God. He said he wasn't going to stop smoking but thanked me for telling him. I saw Mike every summer for a few years after that time and noticed he was still smoking. Hank and I have since changed our summer plans so I don't expect to see Mike at that location again.

Sometime in 1996 I saw a vision that I've named Our Human Timeline of Existence. It was a horizontal Timeline. At the very left of this Timeline was the image of an ape. To the immediate right of the ape was the image of the first human. To the immediate right of the human was the iconic image of Leonardo da Vinci's Vitruvian Man. To the right of that image was an extremely long empty area that took up all of the middle part of the Timeline. At the very right end of the Timeline, and the last image, was a great gust of horizontal wind blurring out the whole right end of the Timeline. This vision said to me that we humans are currently into about 20% of our existence from our beginnings on Earth to our end. I couldn't see the end of us because it was just a blur, so I don't know how it would happen, when, or if it would really happen at all. What I did see is that we humans still have many, many more millenniums of existence. There weren't any words or numbers in this vision, only images. I have always believed in this vision. I never doubted its reality or its message to me, which is that Holy Spirit wants me to make this vision public.

In September 2006, Hank showed me a story in our local newspaper of the current Pope Benedict visiting the Veil of Veronica in Italy. Yes, the cloth that Jesus used to wipe his face and miraculously imprint his face on during the walk to his death is currently framed and protected by the Capuchin Monastery in Manoppello, Italy. The Pope's visit took place on September 1, 2006, the 500th Anniversary of the cloth being in this monastery. I was immediately drawn to this story. After reading and researching it, I had a knowing that the man's picture in the article was truly Jesus's face. I have His face all over my home. You can see Jesus's face for yourself. Do a Google search for Holy Face of Manoppello. You'll see a close-up picture of a man's face with bruises on it and his nose looks broken. His mouth is slightly open, revealing his teeth. That's the real face of Jesus of Nazareth.

On January 4, 2007, I was in the kitchen of my home. I like my home orderly and keep everything in its place. It was daytime and I was preparing some food when my eye caught an object on the floor. I looked down and saw a little white square paper wedged up against the dark green wall runner by the floor. I picked up the paper. It was an empty envelope with a gold lining inside. The envelope looked like it had been opened after it was sealed, as there was a little rip in the flap. It was the kind of envelope that contained a card with someone's name on it that you'd give with a present at Christmas. On the front of the envelope was the hand-printed word *Dad*. It looked like my handwriting but I didn't remember ever giving my father this envelope. And my father had passed on 11 years previously. In my home, an obscure object just doesn't turn up mysteriously in a strange place like that. I stood there with that same shocked feeling, staring at the envelope. I knew where it came from but, again, I needed to rule out all possibilities. I called Hank down into the kitchen. I showed him the envelope and asked if it was his. He said *No*. Did he ever see this before? *No*. Could he imagine where it came from? *No*. I told him where I found it and that it came from Holy Spirit. This time Hank became agitated and got a little angry. He was annoyed that these things were happening and darted back upstairs to his office. I stood there looking at the word *Dad* and asked out loud, *Dad, are you here with me now?* Suddenly, a brisk wind came across my bare shins and I felt the chills. I knew my father was with me.

But I wanted to know more about all of this, so I called a cousin of Hank's who was a deacon at a Catholic church in New Orleans. I asked Gary what all this meant. He said that God made my father my Guardian Angel and that my father would be watching over me. This was awesome. I love my father and was happy to know he would always be with me.

Around November 2009, I attended a funeral of the popular leader of my Bible Study group, David Corley. He was about 50 years old and suffered a heart attack. The large church was packed with coworkers, neighbors, friends, family and his wife and two sons. His former and beloved pastor was giving a eulogy, when I looked up and saw something strange. Suspended in midair was a contained, wavy current of air, hovering in the space between the people and the ceiling, near the front of the church where the casket was. The wavy air area was oval shaped, like a football, and was about six feet long. It didn't move around or do anything special. The wavy air just hovered. At the time I didn't think about what I saw. The next day I thought about it and I knew that that current of wavy air was David's soul attending his own funeral to be with his loved ones and his wife and sons. I wrote a note to his wife, who was a pastor, and an email to everyone I knew who attended David's funeral to tell them that David's soul was at his funeral. I didn't get back any responses.

This vision is particularly and excitedly important because it proved to me two things: that we humans really do have a soul because I saw it with my very own eyes. And, also, the big truth is that we humans don't really die. Yes, our physical bodies die but our eternal soul passes on. So, in truth, we don't totally die. I found this realization comforting and I try to tell as many people as I can that they don't really die. As a result of this experience, I try not to use the word die anymore when someone passes.

CHAPTER 7
The Spokes and The Hub of a Wheel

To continue my story of exploring churches, a friend recommended that I try an Episcopal church. I started going to a High Episcopal church which used incense and had many crucifixes in the sanctuary, about eight. I was loving Jesus up there on the cross, then. I loved the incense, going up to the altar for communion, the priest in full regalia, the musty smell of religion, all the Christian artifacts around. But I was there for only three months. I didn't understand the archaic British selections of reading in Bible Study and there weren't many people going to this church. *This church is religious and interesting but too strange,* so I moved on.

I lost my mind and decided to check out a Catholic church. I say this because I'm a devout Feminist, a Liberal Democrat, an individualist, so I was doomed from the start. I even joined in the Legion of Mary meetings and learned how to pray the rosary. They wouldn't let me take communion because I wasn't a formal Catholic. Silly me, so I joined a conversion class. Nine months of this class, they said, then I could become a Catholic, if they so chose to accept me. I was there two months and left.

At this point I'd like to tell you that throughout my spiritual journey the concepts of evil, satan, hell, devil, sin and original sin didn't resonate with me. I never believed in any of that. I know these things are in the Bible and many people do believe in them but I never bought into the fear and guilt that some people like to try to instill in order to believe in that stuff. I believe that evil things are really just bad things and that evil people are just people doing bad things. That's all. I don't believe there's a place called hell or heaven, for that matter. As for places, I do believe strongly in Eternity, which I guess can be heaven, and which, to me, is all good. I believe that we humans are tempted to do bad things but not by a creature but because we are tempted to do both good and bad things. Sometimes we choose the good things and sometimes we choose the bad things. The choice is always up to each one of us.

That day in my car, I also came to believe that each and every human being's life is pre-determined by God and that Jesus does, indeed, know every hair on our head. I have no problem accepting that God is quite capable of conceiving and performing this grand design. But I also believe that a human being has free will. Hank doesn't understand how I can believe in both these things at the same time. It is hard to explain. I feel that we have free will but that God also has a master plan for each of us.

I want to say something about all the many different religions and beliefs in the world, each claiming to be the One. I received a vision that explained this confusion to me. Spirituality is like a wheel with many spokes. Each spoke represents a religion or belief but all the spokes are going in the same direction—to the hub, to Eternal Being.

Now getting back to churches... Next I joined a liberal, regular Episcopal church in Croton. I was there for a year. They offered a Bible Study class, which I took part in. It was a strange class. The pastor told me it wasn't a traditional Bible Study but a *deconstruction* Bible Study. I sat there in his office and cried at the word *deconstruction*. Here I was, still in love with God and Christianity, tending to the garden of my new roots, builder of my new house in God, and the pastor was talking about *deconstruction*. I told him I was still *constructing* and wanted to leave the group. But I also really wanted to leave this church.

I tried another Episcopal church in Scarborough. It was a very pretty stone church on the grounds of a golf course in a country club. I really joined because it was such a pretty church and on such beautiful grounds, but I'm no golfer. They had a new pastor who was a former marine. He was not a good fit and people started leaving left and right. I was nervous at all the defections. Then the new leader of the Episcopal Church of the United States said in such words that Jesus wasn't so important to Christians and that we shouldn't take His words so seriously. This leader sounded New Age. Whoaaaaaa...that pushed me out the door.

My last church was another Episcopal church in Ossining. I went to service every Sunday, cooked at events. Hank also helped out at fundraisers. I joined the altar committee and took Bible Study. This church was a nice church and the people were friendly and active in the community. When Memorial Day rolled around, I learned that Bible Study and other get-togethers would stop for the summer. I felt cut off from my church and found myself adrift, missing my religious connection. I was planning to return to this church in September when something extraordinary happened during the summer that put me on a very new road.

CHAPTER 8
The CPA

Hank and I vacationed every June at a resort in Lenox, Massachusetts. It was a week-long event that offered workshops to the many people who returned year after year. For four years I gave a workshop called *Conversations About God.* This open forum invited people to talk about how they felt about God and about their spiritual experiences. It was not about religion, only God. We talked about the signs we received from God and about miracles we saw or heard about in our personal lives. My goal for this workshop was for us to get close to God and to connect with each other.

On Friday, June 26, 2009 at 1:45pm, I went to a room to conduct my workshop which was to start at 2:00. I was standing by the room's door waiting to greet people as they arrived. A man walked up to me. He was a large man, about 6'2". He had white hair nicely styled...bald on top, longish on the bottom. He wore a geometric-designed tent garment that covered him from neck to knee. His face was clean-shaven with pink shiny cheeks. He had this powerful and pleasant look on his face. But I was struck by his face because it was glowing. There was an unmistakable glow coming from his face, as if a light was on inside his head. I could see that the glow was of a spiritual nature. I couldn't stop staring at his face and its glow.

I asked this man if he was a minister. I was wondering if he was coming to my workshop for personal or professional reasons. He was friendly and said that he wasn't a minister and that he came for personal reasons. We chatted lightly while waiting for the rest of the people. Normally about 20-25 people came to my workshop each year but it was 2:00 and no one else showed up. We went inside and I set up chairs in a circle. One other man came. He was a regular participant who lived in Boston. We were friendly and teased each other because he was a Red Sox fan and I was a Yankees fan. By 2:15 I could see no one else was coming. I thought it was strange. Not even Hank came that day and he came to all my other workshops.

This man and I immediately locked into each other, talking spiritually. I don't really remember all that we talked about. That part of the conversation was blocked from my mind. The Boston man tried to talk with us but we totally ignored him, though not with malice, so he got up and left. The man and I continued our conversation.

Then this stranger said to me, "You're an E.T. Master."

I looked at him for a long while. I took him seriously, that's the strange part. "What's an E.T.?" I cautiously asked.

He paused, staring at me, "You know, an extraterrestrial."

My spirit and my eyes were locked with his spirit and his eyes. "Oh," I think I said.

"I'm an Angel," he matter-of-factly said to me.

I believed him. I believed everything he was telling me. I wasn't afraid of him and I didn't think he was crazy. I trusted and totally believed this total stranger. That's what's so strange.

"I didn't even want to come up here," he said. "I have work to do and a wife and children back home in Texas. I wasn't even planning to come to your workshop. I was sleeping but a loud noise woke me up so I looked on the agenda to see what workshops were scheduled. I saw your workshop and decided to come. Now I know that I was sent here to see you."

"What's your name?" I asked.

"You can call me Fred."

"What work do you do?"

"I'm a CPA."

"What am I supposed to do? What are you saying to me? I don't understand. Are there books I should read?"

He looked away from me and said: "You will be meeting people. They will show you the way."

I don't remember what else we talked about in the one to two hours we talked. But I do remember that I was spiritually locked into him, like I was spiritually locked into the glow and cross and the ghost.

He got up to leave and said goodbye. I said goodbye but I didn't get up. I couldn't get up. I was just sitting there, numb, just staring ahead. He stopped and turned around, "Are you okay?"

"Yes, I'm okay," was all I could say.

I sat alone in the room not really thinking about anything. At some point I got up and returned to Hank. I told him a little bit about my unusual workshop but I didn't tell him then what Fred said to me.

Later that night I saw Fred one more time at a dance our event put on. As soon as I saw him I went over to give him a big hug and a kiss on the cheek and I said thank you. He smiled. He didn't say anything, though. We parted and I went back to Hank and we danced the night away. I remember looking for Fred in the dance room later on but I never saw him again.

I regret not knowing his last name or not asking for his contact information. I tried to find out more about him so I could contact him but the organizers of the event couldn't help me without a last name.

When the event was over, my husband and I returned home and I waited for these people I was supposed to meet.

CHAPTER 9
Jesus's Other Book

It was July. I was missing my religious connection to a church. I happened to be talking with a friend who invited me to join a spiritual group who met every week in her home. She had been asking me for years to come check out her group, *A Course in Miracles*, but I always said no. This time I said yes.

I went to her comfortable home on Wednesday afternoon at 4:00pm. There were five women and one man sitting in the living room. We sat in a circle and introduced ourselves. When it was the man's turn to say his name, he said his name was *Fred*. I felt connected to that name and knew in an instant that these were the people I was supposed to meet. I was meant to learn about *A Course in Miracles*.

Excitedly, I told everyone about my experience with the other Fred and that I felt I was meant to be in this group. I felt the chills again while saying all this. I always know I'm connected to God when I get the chills.

The people in the group told me what ACIM was and how it got started. What they said was pretty amazing. No, I mean *really amazing!* They gave me a two-inch-thick hardcover book with that name on its cover. They said the book was "written" by Jesus who channeled His words through a Columbia University professor of psychology named Helen Schucman. She scribed His words from 1965-1972.

Funny, I was believing all they told me, though I was surprised that I didn't hear about this book before. I thought the Bible was the only book that Jesus "wrote" in. These people and ACIM were who and what I was waiting for to take me on the next leg of my spiritual journey.

To be honest with you, my time studying *A Course in Miracles* was a strange one. All throughout my learning, I had a lot of trouble understanding Jesus's words and message. The words were in English but it was as if He spoke in another language. His thoughts and directives, to me, were not direct and easy to understand but conceptual and abstract. I always had trouble understanding that kind of talking or reading. Every once in a while in my ACIM learning I had an *Aha!* moment and I got what He was saying. Those moments made me realize I was truly learning something.

One time I was reading a passage and a phrase came up about being up in outer space and I started to cry. I visualized myself in outer space and just burst out crying. The two veteran members of ACIM looked at me and they both smiled. While I was crying, they were smiling. I said to them, "*Why are you smiling when I'm crying?*" but they didn't answer me.

The miracles that Jesus was talking about in this study is that any time you move away from ego and go into Spirit, is a miracle. Any time you move away from pain and go into Peace, is a miracle. Any time you move away from hatred and go into Love, is a miracle. Spirit. Peace. Love. That's what *A Course in Miracles* is all about. You can have a big whopping miracle one day and dozens of little miracles another day. Not talking highly of yourself but being humble is a miracle. You're choosing Spirit over ego. Not taking a dig at your spouse but being patient is a miracle. You're choosing Peace over pain. Not honking your car horn when someone cuts you off but being tolerant is a miracle. You're choosing Love over hate. That's what *A Course In Miracles* is all about.

I've experienced big and little miracles. They happen with my husband, Hank, with friends, with strangers, with the people in my Miracles group, with myself. My awareness was the thing that helped me to recognize that a miracle was being offered to me. I would become aware of this offering and then I'd ask myself, *Do I do the same old thing or do I change and act the right way?*

Sometime near the end of my learning I was growing bored and irritable with the book. I didn't understand what I was reading at all or what other people were saying when they read. I thought it was so repetitious, that Jesus was saying the same simple message over and over in thousands of different ways. Choose Spirit, Peace and Love, not ego. I felt I understood it. I got it. I kept saying out loud to Jesus in the group, *Okay, I get it! I get it! Now what?* I mean, I know that now it's up to me to do the work.

During this teaching I became aware of things and people that were new to me and key to my next spiritual awareness.

I learned about quantum physics. I had not heard about this science. According to ACIM, roughly speaking, quantum physics proves that nothing is real. In such words, that tiny quantum particles that are contained within atoms have so much air and space around them that the animal, vegetable or mineral containing them is not really a solid. That there are really no solids in life, that we humans are not solid and not real. I felt a deep sense of awe learning this.

Because of quantum physics I became even more interested than I already was in outer space and in the universe. I felt a connection to our space program ever since the 1950s when we began to launch rockets into outer space. I watched and read about almost every rocket and spacecraft launch that America has had. I think it is so exciting.

During ACIM, I also became interested in and excited by Deepak Chopra's teachings. I fell totally in love. I heard about him since the 70s but I didn't understand what he was saying. All of a sudden, because of ACIM, I developed an understanding of Chopra's teachings. I read his books *Reinventing the Body, Resurrecting the Soul* and *The Third Jesus*. I loved those books and understood every word. Everything he said resonated with me. Chopra opened my mind to a higher level, I feel. He also helped me to know why I couldn't understand Jesus's words in the ACIM book. To the best of my knowledge I remember Chopra saying that there were about 12 levels of consciousness. That we ordinary humans were on the lowest levels and that Jesus, being God, is on the upper-most level. So my rational brain told me that Jesus's words and concepts were difficult to comprehend because they were written by God who was on the highest level of consciousness and I was on a much lower level. That made sense to me.

I felt I reached the end of the road at ACIM so I stopped going to the meetings, even though I didn't know where I would go next.

CHAPTER 10
The Untethered Soul

I was in a spiritual store one day, browsing their books. I found myself drawn to a book entitled *The Untethered Soul* by Michael Singer. On the front cover was a simple image of a beach, the ocean and a lone black horse on the beach. I was drawn to the cover image's simplicity and to the lone black horse. At the top was a simple and good review by Deepak Chopra, which instantly made me want to buy it, which I did.

I started reading it and felt an immediate connection. Every word resonated with me. I was Home again. As of this writing, I'm almost finished reading it and I don't want it to end. I read one or two pages at a time and then think about its deep message for a day or two. I love it. I know I'm on the right path.

This path is about consciousness and letting go. And about Eternity. I can't even write too much about this whole thing because it's still very new to me. I don't even know the words to use to describe it to you. I do know that I love Eternity. I believe that when I pass on, I will go into Eternity. I am drawn to the universe and outer space. I believe in UFOs and that there's life on other planets.

I attended a past-life workshop recently, out of curiosity, to see what would happen. As the leader used her tools to get us to go back into our past during a trance, we were supposed to go through a door and visit a past life but I saw an open window and I flew out. I flew right into outer space. I remember flying around in a dark universe and feeling happy and free. I was alone doing this but I remember seeing a couple of people. One of them I think was Hank. I don't know how long I was there but I was awakened by the leader who was coaxing me to wake up. I remember it was an effort to get myself back into the present world. When I regained my senses, she told me she thought I was asleep because I looked to be in a deep state. I told her about my experience but she didn't say anything about it.

CHAPTER 11
Eternity

I understand that the title of my book, *God Is Real, My Spiritual Journey to God and Eternity*, contain really big words. But I can say with 100% certainty that I have found God and that God is real. But Eternity, well, I'm still going toward it and trying to understand it. I don't even know if I found a little bit of Eternity here on Earth.

I think I must end my book here. I'm so very new to the world of consciousness that, like I said, I can't even talk about it. My dear friend, Barbara, who also attended ACIM with me, recently asked me what the difference was between *A Course in Miracles* and what I was reading in *The Untethered Soul*. I stood there and didn't really know what to say. I couldn't explain the difference because I didn't know it yet. Is what I'm learning now really all about Eternal Being and Eternity? What else is it about? I hope to find out and maybe write a second book and tell you what I've learned.

I wish you successful finds in your own search for God and Eternity.

The End

Photo: Hank Teller

Award-Winning Author/Artist Shelley Gilbert creates and publishes original fiction and nonfiction books for adults, young adults and children.

Fiction
1. *Land of Sooj, Six Seahorse Stories*, 2011
2. *Swimming Naked with Jellyfish*, 2008

Nonfiction
3. *God Is Real, My Spiritual Journey to God and Eternity*, 2012
4. *Islands, A Coloring Book for Adults, 2ⁿᵈ Edition, 30 Hand-Drawn Drawings, 30 Poems*, 2011
5. *Islands, A Coloring Book for Adults, Volume 2, 30 Hand-Drawn Drawings, 30 Poems*, 2011
6. *Islands, A Coloring Book for Teens and Kids, 30 Hand-Drawn Drawings, 30 Poems and Recipes*, 2010
7. *Islands, A Coloring Book for Adults, 30 Drawings, 30 Poems*, 2001

A visual artist, her collage is award-winning and her tape paintings showed in Madison Avenue art galleries juried competitions. She was also a secretary, taxi driver, sign engraver, jewelry maker and gift shop owner/operator. Born in Brooklyn, NY, the author graduated from SUNY Empire State College, NY/Creative Writing and The Publishing Institute, University of Denver, CO. She lives in New York with her husband Hank Teller.

Facebook: http://tiny.cc/wick9
Website: www.shelleyjoygilbert.com
Email: shelley@shelleyjoygilbert.com

www.ingramcontent.com/pod-product-compliance
Lightning Source LLC
Chambersburg PA
CBHW060545030426
42337CB00021B/4433